Tough Topics

Safety Around the House

Ana Deboo

Heinemann

www.heinemann.co.uk/library

Visit our website to find out more information about Heinemann Library books.

To order:

☎ Phone 44 (0) 1865 888066

▤ Send a fax to 44 (0)1865 314091

▭ Visit the Heinemann Library Bookshop at www.heinemann.co.uk/library to browse our catalogue and order online.

Editorial: Charlotte Guillain
Design: Richard Parker and Q2A Solutions
Picture Research: Erica Martin and Ginny Stroud-Lewis
Production: Duncan Gilbert

Originated by Chroma Graphics (Overseas) Pte. Ltd
Printed and bound in China by South China Printing Co.Ltd

ISBN 978 0 431 90776 5 (hardback)
11 10 09 08 07
10 9 8 7 6 5 4 3 2 1

ISBN 978 0 431 90781 9 (paperback)
12 11 10 09 08
10 9 8 7 6 5 4 3 2 1

British Library Cataloguing in Publication Data
Deboo, Ana
Safety Around the House. - (Tough topics)
1. Home accidents - Juvenile literature 2. Home accidents - Prevention - Juvenile literature
I. Title
363.1'3

A full catalogue record for this book is available from the British Library.

Acknowledgements
The author and publisher are grateful to the following for permission to reproduce copyright material: Alamy Images pp. 6 (Ian Shaw), 11 (Sciencephotos), 18 (AcestockLimited); Art Directors and Trip pp. 7, 8, 14, 16, 20, 23, 27; Corbis pp. 4 (John-Francis Bourke/Zefa), 9, 13 (Randy Faris), 17, 21 (Shannon Fagan), 28 (Zefa/S. Oskar); Getty Images pp. 5 (Taxi/David Seed Photography), 10 (DK Images/Ian O'Leary), 12 (Stone/Jonathan Kantor), 19 (Stone), 22 (Photographer's Choice), 24 (Taxi/Simon Watson), 26 (Stone/Andreas Pollok); Mediscan p. 29; Science Photo Library p. 25 (Michael Donne).

Cover photograph reproduced with permission of Getty Images/ Taxi/ David Seed Photography.

Every effort has been made to contact copyright holders of any material reproduced in this book. Any omissions will be rectified in subsequent printings if notice is given to the publishers.

Disclaimer
All the Internet addresses (URLs) given in this book were valid at the time of going to press. However, due to the dynamic nature of the Internet, some addresses may have changed, or sites may have changed or ceased to exist since publication. While the author and publishers regret any inconvenience this may cause readers, no responsibility for any such changes can be accepted by either the author or publishers.

Contents

Some words are shown in bold, **like this**. You can find out what they mean by looking in the glossary.

Accidents at home

Home is a place where people usually feel safe from danger. But accidents are common in homes, even for teenagers and adults.

▼Learning about household dangers will help you avoid them.

4

▲ Cookers and pots stay hot for a while after the heat is turned off.

Some household items are dangerous to drink or even touch, such as bleach and oven cleaner. Some objects can cause physical **injury**, such as knives and hot cookers.

Household supplies

Nearly every home contains cleaning supplies. People often have other products in their homes that contain harmful **chemicals**, such as paints, **pesticides**, and weed killers.

▶ It is important to use cleaning products safely.

▲ Do not touch any household products you are not familiar with.

Many household chemicals are **poisonous**. Some, such as pesticides or cleaning products, can kill people or make them very ill.

Dangerous chemicals

Household products are used to clean floors, bathrooms, and **appliances**. Many contain **chemicals** that can harm your skin. Some, like drain cleaners, can cause **chemical burns**.

◄ Never let household products touch your skin unless you know they are safe to use.

▲ Washing-up liquid is safe
to touch. Gloves will help
keep your skin from drying

Household chemicals can also cause
rashes or other skin irritations. If you
accidentally get a household cleaner on
your skin or in your eyes, wash the area
immediately and tell an adult.

Harmful fumes

▶ Mix paints outside or where there is plenty of fresh air.

Household products such as paints and paint cleaners give off dangerous **fumes**. These gases are harmful to breathe in. They can cause headaches and can harm the brain and lungs.

▶When bleach is mixed with ammonia or vinegar, it creates a poisonous gas.

Never mix household products together. Some combinations can create **poisonous** fumes or cause explosions.

Medicines and vitamins

▶ Get an adult's permission before taking any medicine.

Medicines and **vitamins** are helpful when taken correctly, but they can be **poisonous** if you take too much. The iron in some multivitamins for adults can be poisonous to young people.

Many people **overdose** by guessing how much medicine to take. Always follow the instructions when taking a medicine, and never take a medicine with somebody else's name on it. That medicine is a **prescription drug**. It was chosen by a doctor for that person only.

▲ Always measure the amount of medicine you take.

Warning labels

Before using any product, always read the label on the package. The label explains how to use the product, tells of possible dangers, and gives **first aid** instructions in case there is an accident.

◄ Medicine labels warn of side effects such as drowsiness.

CAUTION: Use with adequate ventilation. In case of eye contact, flush immediately with water for at least 15 minutes.

WARNING: Causes eye and skin irritation. Do not get in eyes, on skin, or on clothing.

⚠ DANGER

CONTENTS ARE FLAMMABLE: Keep spray away from heat, sparks, pilot lights, open flames, etc. Unplug electrical tools, motors, and other appliances before spraying or bringing the can near any source of electricity.

◄ "Caution," "Warning," and "Danger" are words to look for.

Many products have warning labels that tell you how to use the product safely. "Caution" means the product could cause health problems. "Warning" means it could cause more serious health problems or catch fire. "Danger" means it could explode or cause serious injury or death.

Inhalants

Sometimes people breathe in the **fumes** from glue or household **chemicals** on purpose. This makes them feel dizzy for a few seconds. Some people enjoy this feeling and do not realize the fumes can harm their bodies.

▶Breathing in harmful fumes can cause brain damage that cannot be reversed.

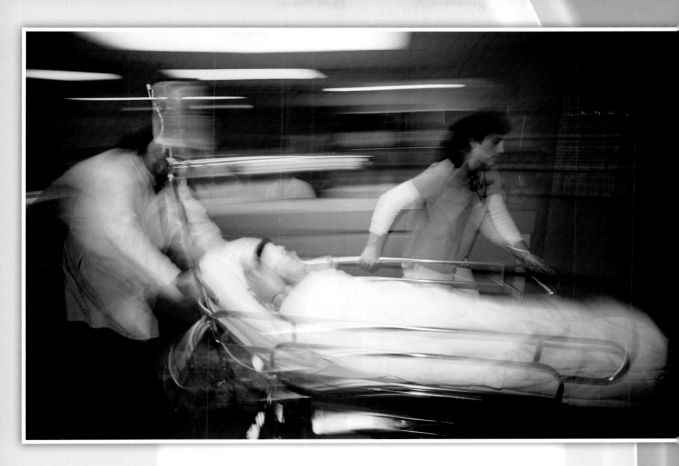

▲Using inhalants can be deadly.

Inhalants can damage the brain, liver, kidneys, eyes, and ears. The fumes from some chemicals can cause the heart to stop beating. They can also cause a person to **suffocate** and die.

Carbon monoxide

◄ Never leave a car engine running in a closed space.

The most common cause of accidental poisoning is **carbon monoxide** gas. Heaters, fireplaces, tumble dryers, barbecues, and car engines all give off carbon monoxide. If carbon monoxide collects in a room or garage, it can quickly leave a person **unconscious** or dead.

You cannot see or smell carbon monoxide, so it is important to be careful around things that make it. Fresh air should be allowed into rooms where heaters or dryers are being used. You can also install a special alarm that can tell when there are dangerous levels of carbon monoxide.

▶One of the first signs of carbon monoxide poisoning is a headache.

Flammable substances

Some household products give off **fumes** that are very **flammable**. They can cause fires. Keep plenty of fresh moving air in the room when using these items.

▶ Products such as hair spray, nail varnish remover, and oven cleaner give off flammable gases.

▲ Scents are added to natural gas and propane so people can smell a leak.

Natural gas and propane are used as fuels for some cookers. They can cause fires or explosions if there is a leak and the fumes get trapped in a room. If you smell gas in a room, do not turn on any light switches. Leave the room and find an adult immediately.

Electrical appliances

◄ Broken electrical devices can cause fires if they overheat or begin to spark.

Electricity powers many objects in a home. Electricity can also give people a **shock**, causing uncomfortable tingling, burns, or even death. If an **appliance** does not work well or the electrical cord looks damaged, do not use it.

Never stick any object into a wall socket or into appliances such as a toaster. Also, be sure to keep appliances away from water. Electricity travels easily through water, increasing the chance of an electrical shock.

▶Appliances such as hair dryers should never be used near sinks or bath tubs.

Appliances that get hot

Be careful around **appliances** that get hot, such as cookers, heaters, and irons. These heat sources can cause fires and burns.

◄ Use a cooker with the help of an adult.

◄ Putting cloth items on top of heaters or lamps can cause house fires.

Be on the alert for other things that heat up, too. Lightbulbs get very hot and can burn you if you touch them. Never put anything on top of a lightbulb or lamp. It could catch fire.

Sharp tools

▲ When using a knife, make sure you do not rush or get distracted.

When you use sharp knives, always handle them correctly. Never play with them, wave them in the air, or touch a knife you do not have permission to use.

Tools such as saws, chisels and pliers can be dangerous. They can have very sharp edges and must be used with care. You should only use gardening tools such as shears, secateurs and spades when you have an adult to help you.

▶ Alway ask an adult to show you how to use tools.

What to do in an emergency

When accidents do happen, reacting quickly is important. Learn the emergency services telephone number—999—by heart.

▲ Ask an adult to put a list of emergency numbers near the telephone.

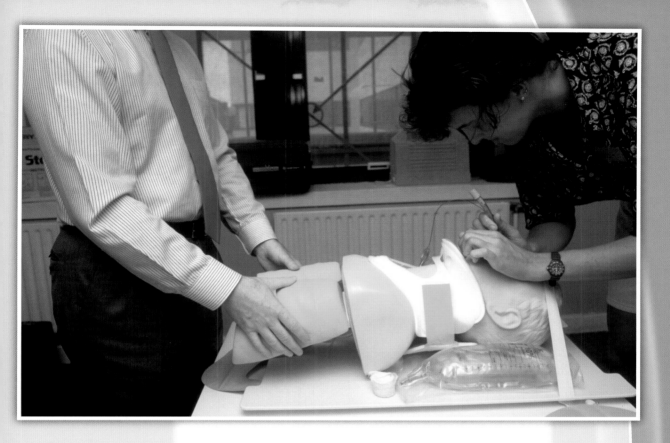

▲Special classes teach **first aid**.

If you have to call an emergency number, be ready to tell the operator your name, exactly what is wrong, and your address. Learning about the dangers in your home can help avoid accidents. Learning how to react in an emergency can help save lives.

Glossary

appliance household machine, such as a dishwasher or toaster

carbon monoxide poisonous gas that is produced during the process of burning

chemical substance that can be created by or is used in scientific processes

chemical burn injury caused by contact with a chemical

first aid care given to a sick or injured person before medical help arrives

flammable able to catch fire quickly

fume smoke or gas that is usually harmful

inhalant chemical fumes that are breathed in

injury damage to the body

overdose take too much of a drug

pesticide chemical that kills pests such as cockroaches, mice, or rats

poisonous able to cause injury or death if taken into the body

prescription drug drug chosen by a doctor for a patient

shock passage of electricity through the body. Electrical shocks can cause burns, unconsciousness, or death.

suffocate to die as a result of not being able to breathe

unconscious unable to see, hear, or know what is happening around you

vitamin chemical that the body needs to stay healthy

Find out more

Books to read

Look Out: At Home by Claire Llewellyn (Hodder Wayland, 2006)

Healthy Choices: Keeping Safe by Cath Senker (Hodder Wayland, 2004)

Look out at Home by Helena Ramsay (Evans Brothers Ltd, 2003)

Websites

- The Royal Society for the Prevention of Accidents (ROSPA) has a website that tells you how to stay safe at home and when you are out and about. Find out more at www.rospa.com.

- The Children's Safety Education Foundation has created a website with information for children at www.csef.net.

- Kidshealth.org (www.kidshealth.org/kid) has information on health and safety topics.

- Child Safety Week takes place every June in the UK. Find out more about it at www.capt.org.uk/csweek.

Index